COMMAND YOUR WEALTH

COMMAND YOUR WEALTH

THE EXECUTIVE'S BLUEPRINT FOR FINANCIAL CLARITY AND SUCCESS

NICHOLAS OLESEN, CFP®, CPWA®

Command Your Wealth

ISBN (paperback): 979-8-9997822-0-5
ISBN (hardcover): 979-8-9997822-3-6
ISBN (ebook): 979-8-9997822-1-2
ISBN (audiobook): 979-8-9997822-2-9

Editorial services: Sandra Wendel, Write On, Inc.
Design: Marko Markovic, 5mediadesign

Published by Kathmere Capital Management
Contact the author at *nolesen@kathmere.com* or *www.kathmere.com*

Disclaimer

do not ensure or guarantee better performance and cannot eliminate the risk of investment losses.

Projections are based on assumptions that may not come to pass. They do not reflect the impact that advisory fees and other investment-related expenses will have on the value of an investor's portfolio.

CONTENTS

INTRODUCTION

After nearly two decades working with successful executives, entrepreneurs, and professionals, I've witnessed a recurring theme: Even the most accomplished leaders often feel overwhelmed or uncertain about their financial lives. They, like you, are experts in their careers, but when it comes to compensation, taxes, estate planning, or legacy goals, they're often unsure where to start or whom to trust.

That's why I wrote this book.

I want to help you think about how to navigate complex equity packages, build intentional wealth plans, and align your resources with your deepest values. My goal in sharing this book is simple: to empower you with the clarity, tools, and mindset needed to take control of your financial life—and to do so in a way that brings confidence, freedom, and purpose.

Command Your Wealth is not about theory. It's about real-world decisions, real-life stories, and proven strategies that lead to financial success and true alignment of your capital and values. Whether you're negotiating your next comp package, receiving a new equity grant and don't know what to do, planning a sabbatical, or preparing your family for the future, I hope this guide serves as your trusted blueprint.

Let's begin.

1

THE UNIQUE FINANCIAL LIFE OF AN EXECUTIVE

MARK SAT ACROSS FROM ME IN the conference room, his brow furrowed and arms crossed over a folder of recent paperwork. He was just promoted to senior vice president at a Fortune 500 company, and his compensation had skyrocketed—and so had the complexity of his financial life. Between performance-based stock options, deferred compensation, a cash bonus with clawback provisions, and new fiduciary obligations, he looked more overwhelmed than excited.

"I know I should be thrilled," he said, "but I have no idea what any of this actually means for my future."

This story is not unique. In fact, it's one I've heard from countless high-performing professionals stepping into senior leadership roles. The truth is, success in your career often brings with it a level of financial complexity that most traditional financial planning tools—and certainly DIY approaches—simply aren't equipped to handle. For corporate executives, the road to wealth isn't just paved with higher paychecks. It's littered with equity compensation plans, tax traps, reputational risk, and legal fine print.

But beyond the paperwork and spreadsheets lies a deeper tension—an internal conflict between outward success and internal confidence. You may, like Mark, be confident you've mastered your profession, only to feel like an amateur when it comes to managing your wealth. This disconnect isn't just frustrating—it's emotionally taxing.

The Executive Complexity Curve

When you're promoted into leadership, you enter what I call the Executive Complexity Curve. At first glance, the rewards of the position—more income, greater autonomy, prestige—seem like the end goal. But almost immediately, the accompanying financial decisions outpace the simplicity of just saving more.

Suddenly, you're making decisions about when to exercise stock options, how to allocate your investments without becoming overly concentrated in your company stock, how to defer income or reduce taxes, and what kind of trust structures you might need to protect your growing estate.

Unlike paychecks for salaried professionals, your compensation isn't simply direct deposit and a 401(k). You may often have these features:

- Equity compensation with vesting schedules that affect your liquidity and taxable income
- Deferred compensation plans that push income into future years—often with distribution and risk considerations
- High marginal tax rates that require strategic timing of income and deductions
- Concentrated stock exposure that ties both your career and your wealth to your employer's performance
- Complex estate needs because of illiquid or nontransferable assets

And let's consider your time scarcity—you're too busy to manage it all alone.

This complexity doesn't just affect your financial statements—it impacts your sense of stability and control. Mark, like many executives, thought he was just receiving a promotion. What he didn't realize was that he'd entered a new chapter in his financial life—one that demanded a new approach and a new mindset.

The Psychological Weight of Wealth

Most people assume financial success leads to peace of mind. But for many executives, the opposite is often true. With more at stake, more moving parts, and more people relying on you, your mental burden can increase dramatically.

You report higher levels of financial anxiety than many expect. Not because you don't earn enough, but because the stakes are so high—and so personally tied to your identity. When your company stock drops, it doesn't just hurt your portfolio. It can feel like a judgment on your leadership. When you're unsure about your tax strategy or estate plan, it may feel like you're failing to protect your family.

You also can pay an emotional toll in trying to keep up appearances. You may feel pressure to "have it all together" because of your title, when in reality you're juggling financial decisions you've never faced before—often in silence. I've seen this lead to sleepless nights, increased tension at home, and a persistent undercurrent of guilt or insecurity, especially among those who feel you should "know better."

In one client conversation, a seasoned executive confided:

> "Everyone assumes I've got this figured out.
> I don't. And I'm too embarrassed to admit it."

Acknowledging that complexity is normal—and that asking for help is wise, not weak—is often the first breakthrough.

Why Traditional Planning Falls Short

Most financial advice is built around two principles: budgeting and retirement savings. While these are valid for many households, they are rarely sufficient for executives. Let's look at a few key reasons:

- Your income is not stable or predictable: Bonuses, performance shares, and stock options create variability in both cash flow and taxable income.
- Your assets are not liquid: A significant portion of your net worth may be in restricted stock, options, or deferred compensation, limiting flexibility.
- You face unique tax exposures: Alternative Minimum Tax (AMT), Net Investment Income Tax (NIIT), and multi-state taxation may all be part of your reality.
- You may be subject to insider trading rules: This limits when you can buy or sell shares, creating a planning challenge.
- You may become a public figure: Even if your name isn't in the press, your decisions can carry reputational risk for both you and your company.

What you need isn't just investment advice or tax filing assistance; you need integrated wealth management that accounts for all these realities and how these decisions impact your life, not just your balance sheet. I call this holistic wealth management and, for executives, it goes well beyond traditional budgeting and savings. Crafting and consistently reviewing your holistic plan is one of the foundational building blocks of financial success.

Case Study: From Confusion to Clarity

When Mark and I first mapped out his financial picture, it was like untangling a knotted ball of yarn. Here's what we discovered:

- He had three different tranches of Restricted Stock Unit (RSUs) with different vesting dates and values.
- His Incentive Stock Option (ISO) grant from five years ago was almost fully vested and in the money.
- He had opted into a 409A deferred compensation plan but hadn't selected distribution schedules.
- His bonus put him in a higher Alternative Minimum Tax (AMT) exposure zone than expected.
- His wife had a small business creating overlapping tax and planning concerns.

We created a comprehensive plan that prioritized these items:

1. Optimizing equity compensation timing to balance liquidity needs and tax efficiency
2. Building a diversified portfolio that reduced his company exposure to under 15% of his net worth
3. Establishing a Donor-Advised Fund (DAF) using appreciated shares to offset Restricted Stock Unit tax consequences
4. Aligning his deferred comp distribution to begin five years post-retirement, reducing his tax bracket
5. Setting up a revocable trust to begin estate planning in a flexible, efficient way

Within six months, Mark went from uncertain and reactive to empowered and proactive. And the change wasn't just financial—it was emotional. He no longer felt like his finances were happening to him. He was in control.

Additional Case: The Cost of Delay

Another client, Danielle, an executive at a biotech firm, put off reviewing her stock option plan for over a year because of back-to-back product launches and board meetings. By the time we reviewed it, one set of her Incentive Stock Options had expired worthless—despite being well in the money—due to the ten-year expiration rule. It wasn't negligence. It was time poverty.

Worse, she hadn't updated her estate plan after a divorce five years earlier. Her former spouse was still listed as the primary beneficiary on a deferred comp plan worth seven figures.

These weren't just financial oversights; they were emotional triggers. The expired options made her feel foolish. The estate error made her feel vulnerable. But after a few months of coordinated action, she regained her footing. The process of getting organized gave her a renewed sense of agency and, more importantly, peace.

Time Scarcity: Your Silent Risk

If there's one universal truth about executives, it's this: You are busy. Your calendar is packed. Your inbox is overflowing. You may be flying cross-country, managing teams, answering to a board, and fielding investor calls—all in a single week. That kind of time constraint is the enemy of intentional planning.

You may delay financial decisions because you feel you can't give them proper attention. But delaying, especially in the context of equity compensation and taxes, can be costly. Consider—

- An unexercised Incentive Stock Option (ISO) can expire worthless after ten years
- A vesting Restricted Stock Unit (RSU) could cause a surprise tax bill in a year with already high income

- Missing a 10b5-1 window could mean you're stuck holding concentrated stock during a market downturn

Time scarcity doesn't just delay planning, it amplifies risk. That's why many executives benefit most from building what we'll later explore as our Efficient Family Office model—where a team of coordinated professionals handles the complexity on your behalf.

About now, you will start seeing terms with plenty of acronyms. It is not my intention to throw a bunch of industry and tax jargon at you. But I am going to use terms you should get to know. I'll explain every concept and every term when I introduce them. For further reference, I have included a glossary at the back of the book.

A Shift in Perspective: From Earners to Stewards

As you move up in leadership, it's not just your paycheck that grows. Your influence, responsibility, and reach expand as well. That same shift should happen in your mindset around money.

Think of your role not only as an earner, but as a steward of your wealth. That means being intentional with how you handle the following:

- Allocate your resources
- Protect your family
- Support causes you believe in
- Communicate your financial values to your children or heirs

For many executives, wealth creates the possibility of legacy—but legacy doesn't just happen. It's built, brick by brick, through decisions that align with your values. That's why emotional clarity and financial strategy must work hand in hand.

As one client said to me after finally setting up her estate plan: "I thought I was just organizing my documents. But it felt like I was writing a letter to the future."

Looking Ahead

The rest of this book is designed to give you the clarity and confidence you need to take control of your wealth. You'll learn how to

- Make sense of your compensation,
- Strategically manage taxes,
- Invest wisely given your unique circumstances,
- Plan for your legacy with intention, and
- Create a life where work is optional—and purpose is central.

Each chapter builds on the last, providing stories, examples, tools, and action steps tailored to your situation as an executive. Whether you're midcareer or nearing retirement, this journey begins with one foundational truth:

Your financial life is different.
Your plan should be too.

2

CRACK THE CODE: MAKING SENSE OF EXECUTIVE PAY

SUSAN, A NEWLY APPOINTED VP OF clinical strategy at a rapidly growing biotech company, sat across from me with her HR packet spread across the table. She sighed and pushed it forward.

"I think this is a good offer," she said. "But honestly, I don't even understand half of it."

The offer included a base salary, cash bonus, sign-on Restricted Stock Units (RSUs), a ten-year Incentive Stock Option (ISO) grant, and eligibility for the deferred compensation plan and employee stock purchase program. In total, it was a multimillion-dollar package—but to Susan, it was alphabet soup.

This confusion is incredibly common. Companies use equity and performance-based compensation to attract and retain top talent. But for the executives on the receiving end, these plans introduce complexity, risk, and opportunity—all requiring careful navigation. And when these compensation plans are misunderstood or ignored, they often lead to costly mistakes, tax surprises, and underutilized wealth.

Let's break it down and build your confidence in understanding, optimizing, and ultimately mastering your compensation.

Understanding the Components of Executive Compensation

Executive compensation is structured differently from traditional employee pay. While your base salary and bonus are straightforward, the bulk of your compensation—and wealth potential—often comes from these six equity components.

1. **Base Salary and Bonus**

- Typically this is the smallest portion of your total compensation.
- Bonuses may be discretionary or performance-based and are taxed as ordinary income when paid.

Planning Tip: Confirm whether your bonus has clawback provisions or is tied to corporate milestones (often found in offer letters and executive agreements).

2. **Restricted Stock Units (RSUs)**

- Restricted Stock Units are grants of company stock that vest over time (typically over three to four years).
- Taxed as ordinary income upon vesting, RSUs are based on the Fair Market Value of the shares.

Planning Tip: You can't control when RSUs are taxed, but you can decide whether to sell immediately to cover taxes or hold for potential appreciation and long-term capital gains.

3. **Incentive Stock Options (ISOs)**

- Allow you to purchase stock at a fixed exercise price.
- If you meet certain holding requirements (two years from grant, one year from exercise), you qualify for long-term capital gains treatment.
- Trigger Alternative Minimum Tax (AMT) on the spread between exercise price and Fair Market Value (FMV) at the time of exercise.

Planning Tip: Exercise Incentive Stock Options early in the year to provide flexibility and consider Alternative Minimum Tax projections before acting.

Figure 1: Overview of the tax rules for Incentive Stock Options (ISOs). The chart shows how the timing of a sale—relative to the grant date and exercise date—determines whether it is a qualifying or disqualifying disposition, the resulting type of tax owed, and potential Alternative Minimum Tax (AMT) considerations.

4. Non-Qualified Stock Options (NSOs)

- Similar to Incentive Stock Options but do not qualify for favorable tax treatment.
- The spread between exercise price and FMV at exercise is taxed as ordinary income.

Planning Tip: NSOs often trigger immediate tax liability, so plan exercises around your marginal tax bracket and liquidity.

5. Deferred Compensation Plans

- Allow you to defer income into future years (often retirement).
- Deferred income is not currently taxable but is unsecured —meaning, you are essentially lending money to your company.

Planning Tip: Stagger distributions over multiple years to avoid tax bracket "bunching."

6. Employee Stock Purchase Plan (ESPP)

- Offers discounted shares (often 10–15% below market).
- Qualified plans offer favorable tax treatment if holding requirements are met.

Planning Tip: ESPP can be a great tool, but only if you actively track concentration risk and holding period requirements.

Your Quick Tax Guide to Executive Compensation

Compensation Type	Tax Trigger	Tax Type	Special Considerations
RSUs	Vesting	Ordinary income	Cannot defer tax; sell or hold decision needed
ISOs	Exercise (for AMT) + sale (for capital gains)	AMT + capital gains	Long-term gains if held properly
NSOs	Exercise	Ordinary income	Taxed immediately on the spread

Compensation Type	Tax Trigger	Tax Type	Special Considerations
Deferred Comp	Distribution	Ordinary income	Unsecured and exposed to company risk
ESPP	Sale	Ordinary income + capital gains	Holding rules dictate treatment

Case Study: Jason's IPO Trap

Jason, a VP of product at a software company, exercised Incentive Stock Options during a pre-IPO (Initial Public Offering) window, hoping to start the long-term gains clock early. The company went public at a strong valuation, but by the time the six-month lock-up ended, shares had dropped 40%.

Jason still owed Alternative Minimum Tax (AMT) based on the higher valuation at exercise, even though his shares were now worth significantly less. It strained his liquidity and forced him to sell underperforming assets to cover the tax.

Lesson: Align exercise strategy with liquidity events and model downside risk. Early exercise can be powerful—but dangerous without a plan.

Build a Compensation Timeline

Equity comp is not just about what you receive—it's about when and how you act. A well-designed compensation timeline helps you map these items:

- Vesting schedules for Restricted Stock Units (RSUs), Performance Stock Units (PSUs), and options

- Expiration dates for Incentive Stock Options (ISOs) (typically ten years)
- Exercise and tax milestones
- Distribution timelines for deferred compensation
- Liquidity events (IPOs, buyouts, acquisitions)

This timeline becomes your dashboard for proactive planning.

Strategic Planning Methods

Understanding your comp is only half the battle. Here are five proven tactics that transform knowledge into strategy:

1. 10b5-1 Plans

- Prearranged stock sale plans that comply with insider trading rules
- Provide peace of mind and reduce emotional decision-making

2. Net Exercise

- Use shares to pay exercise costs and taxes, minimizing out-of-pocket burden
- Useful for ISOs or Non-Qualified Stock Options with large spreads

3. Charitable Planning

- Donate appreciated shares to Donor-Advised Funds (DAF) to offset income
- Pair with Restricted Stock Unit (RSU) vesting or ISO exercises to neutralize tax impact

Donor-Advised Fund

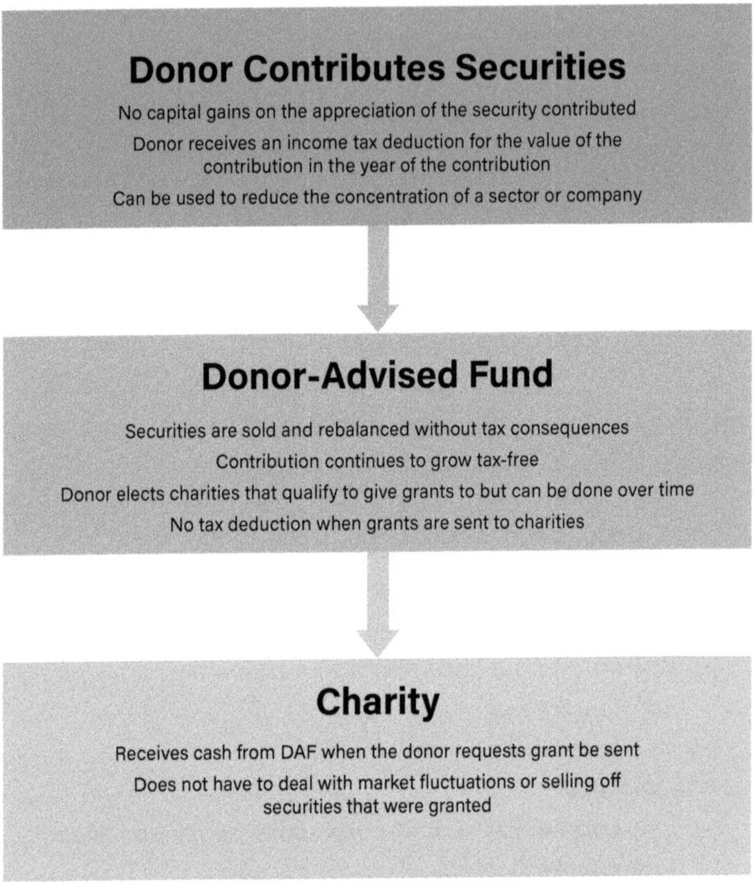

Figure 2: Flow of a Donor-Advised Fund (DAF). This diagram illustrates how appreciated securities can be contributed to a DAF to avoid capital gains taxes and receive an immediate income tax deduction. Within the DAF, assets can be sold, reinvested, and grow tax-free. The donor can recommend grants to eligible charities over time, allowing for flexible giving while providing charities with cash rather than securities.

4. **Diversification via Liquidity Events**

- Gradually reduce concentrated stock positions after vesting or exercising
- Use proceeds to build a more diversified investment portfolio

5. **Hedge Strategies (Advanced)**

- Collars, prepaid variable forward contracts, or exchange funds can reduce risk exposure without immediate sale

Case Study: The Hidden Cost of Ignoring Deferred Comp

David, an executive at a major pharmaceutical firm, elected to defer a significant portion of his annual bonus over eight years but didn't coordinate with his retirement date. His first three years of retirement ended up being the highest-taxed years of his life, thanks to overlapping distributions and severance.

Once we restructured his plan (for future years) and backfilled with Roth conversions and Donor-Advised Fund (DAF) contributions, we were able to significantly reduce his long-term tax exposure.

Lesson: Don't defer income without modeling the distribution phase. Tax deferral doesn't guarantee tax reduction.

Cash Flow vs. Net Worth

You may frequently feel "wealthy on paper but cash poor" because of these reasons:

- Restricted Stock Units and options are illiquid until vested/exercised.

- Deferred comp is inaccessible for years.
- Bonuses may be delayed.
- Tax events drain cash.

To combat this dilemma, you may do the following:

- Maintain elevated cash reserves beyond standard emergency funds.
- Plan RSU sales in advance to create liquidity for taxes and lifestyle needs.
- Use a diversified portfolio to smooth out cash flow between equity events.

Working with an Advisory Team

Optimizing compensation is not a solo sport. You may work with a team made up of these professionals:

- Your wise CPA should model Alternative Minimum Tax (AMT) risk and tax projections for each event.
- A smart financial advisor should build liquidity plans, coordinate sales, and model long-term outcomes.
- And your savvy estate attorney should integrate your equity into trusts, legacy planning, and charitable strategies.

Susan, the biotech VP, had a turning point after we implemented this multipronged strategy:

- Created a 10b5-1 plan for RSU sales during open windows
- Funded a Donor-Advised Fund using high-value shares to reduce tax liability
- Selected staggered deferred comp distributions aligned with her early retirement goals

- Used Roth conversions in low-income years to prepay tax efficiently

What began as alphabet soup to her became a customized engine for building long-term wealth, purpose, and peace of mind.

Final Thoughts

Your compensation package is one of the most powerful engines for building wealth, creating impact, and gaining financial independence—but only if you understand and proactively manage it.

Here's a recap:

- Not all equity is created equal. Learn the difference between Restricted Stock Units (RSUs), Incentive Stock Options (ISOs), Non-Qualified Stock Options (NSOs), Employee Stock Purchase Plans (ESPP), and deferred comp.
- Build a compensation timeline to track vesting, exercise windows, expirations, and tax triggers.
- Coordinate with your CPA, financial advisor, and attorney to develop and execute a holistic plan.
- Use tools like 10b5-1 plans, Donor-Advised Funds, liquidity planning, and hedging to protect and grow your wealth.
- Don't just react. Strategically lead your financial decisions the same way you lead your teams.

The next chapter will dive into how taxes interact with your compensation and how to build strategies to keep more of what you earn.

3

HIGH INCOME, HIGH STAKES: TAX MOVES THAT MATTER

DAVID HAD JUST FINISHED FILING HIS taxes when he called me on the advice of one of my clients. His voice was tight with anxiety.

"I exercised those Incentive Stock Options like I heard I should, but my tax guy just told me I owe $150,000 in Alternative Minimum Tax. Boy, I didn't see that coming. Can you help me?"

To make matters worse, the company's stock had fallen significantly since his exercise, leaving him with a giant tax bill and no liquidity to pay it. It felt like a betrayal. After all, he had followed the textbook strategy and still got burned since he didn't plan ahead or have the right people looking out for him.

David isn't alone. Executive compensation often creates surprise tax liabilities because it's not designed with your actual tax exposure in mind. Most tax software isn't built for this complexity. Many CPAs are trained for compliance, not strategy. The result? Missed opportunities, unnecessary tax bills, and persistent anxiety around year-end.

This chapter will walk you through the major tax principles you need to understand and, more importantly, explain how to take control of your executive tax situation proactively.

The Executive Tax Landscape

High-earning executives live in a different tax world:

- 37% federal marginal income tax
- 3.8% Net Investment Income Tax (NIIT)

- Up to 13.3% in state income taxes (CA, NY, NJ)
- Alternative Minimum Tax exposure due to Incentive Stock Options
- Capital gains layering, especially from stock comp
- Multi-state sourcing and residency traps

When bonuses, equity vesting, deferred comp distributions, and capital gains all collide, it creates massive spikes in taxable income that must be carefully managed.

Case Study 1: Incentive Stock Option Exercise Without Alternative Minimum Tax Planning

David's Incentive Stock Option (ISO) situation is all too common:

- Exercised ISOs in March when stock was at $120 per share
- Fair Market Value triggered $400K in Alternative Minimum Tax (AMT) income
- Stock dropped to $70 per share by December
- No liquidity—but owed $150K in AMT

Better Outcome: If David had exercised early in January, he could've sold the same year for a disqualifying disposition, been taxed under ordinary rates (avoiding Alternative Minimum Tax), and reinvested the proceeds.

Strategy: Incentive Stock Option and Alternative Minimum Tax Management

ISOs are one of the most misunderstood equity types. Their potential is massive—but so is your risk.

Key Concepts

- Incentive Stock Options are not taxed at exercise (for regular tax).
- But the spread is added to Alternative Minimum Tax income.
- If you hold the shares, you could owe AMT regardless of performance.

Planning Strategies

- Run AMT projections before exercise.
- Exercise early in the year so you can sell by year-end if needed.
- If necessary, intentionally disqualify the ISO to trigger ordinary income but preserve liquidity.
- Monitor AMT credit carryforwards to reclaim tax in future years.

Pro Tip: Combine ISO exercises with charitable giving or capital loss harvesting to neutralize the AMT impact.

Restricted Stock Unit (RSUs): The Inescapable Tax Event

Restricted Stock Units are simple in concept—yet potentially disruptive in execution. They automatically vest and trigger ordinary income, with no ability to defer.

Strategies

- Offset RSU income with charitable deductions using Donor-Advised Funds.
- Accelerate deductible expenses like mortgage interest or property tax.

- If RSUs vest during a high-income year, defer bonuses or equity exercises to reduce the stack.

Case Study 2: Charitable Giving as a Tax Lever

Cynthia, a CFO at a public company, had $1.2M in Restricted Stock Units vest in December. She knew it would be a high-tax year, so we did this:

- Contributed $200K in appreciated stock to a Donor-Advised Fund (DAF)
- Bunched charitable deductions into one year to exceed standard deduction limits
- Used proceeds from the RSU sale to rebuild portfolio diversity

Result: She reduced her taxable income by $200K, avoided capital gains on the gifted stock, and preserved liquidity—all while giving more intentionally.

Deferred Compensation: Income Deferral ≠ Tax Avoidance

Deferred comp allows you to delay receiving (and paying tax on) income, usually until retirement. But deferred income is

- Unsecured (at risk if employer goes bankrupt),
- Subject to strict payout schedules once elected, and
- Still taxed by some states even after you move.

Strategic Moves

- Elect multi-year distributions (for example, five or ten years) to avoid bracket spikes.

- Time deferrals to begin post-retirement when income is lower.
- Move to low- or no-income-tax states before distributions begin.
- Don't defer money you'll need in the next five to ten years.

Managing Capital Gains: Timing Is Everything

You may often hold large blocks of low-cost-basis stock. That's good for growth, but dangerous without a tax plan.

Core Tactics

- Hold for 12+ months to qualify for long-term capital gains (15–20%).
- Sell gradually through a 10b5-1 plan.
- Harvest losses to offset gains in volatile years.
- Donate appreciated shares to charity instead of giving cash.

Remember: Long-term capital gains can still trigger NIIT (3.8%) and impact IRMAA (higher monthly Medicare premiums) if not managed.

Multi-State Tax Planning

If you work remotely, travel, or relocate frequently, you can get entangled in multi-state taxation.

State Tax Traps

- States like CA and NY tax-deferred comp earned while living there, even after you move.
- "Days worked" can determine sourcing for bonuses and equity.

- Changing residency takes more than just a move—it requires intentional steps.

Action Plan

- Track days worked in each state.
- Change domicile and primary residence before exercising large grants or retiring.
- Avoid double taxation by consulting with multi-state CPAs.

Executive Charitable Strategy Toolkit

Charitable giving can be more than generous—it can be strategic.

Tool	Benefit	Best For
Donor-Advised Fund (DAF)	Immediate deduction, long-term grantmaking	Annual bonuses, RSUs, appreciated shares
Charitable Remainder Trust (CRT)	Converts stock into income, delays tax	Highly appreciated, concentrated stock
Private Foundation	Long-term family giving, control over grants	Multigenerational wealth and legacy planning
Qualified Charitable Distributions (QCDs)	Direct IRA to charity (age 70½+)	Reducing RMD taxes in retirement

Bonus and Distribution Timing

Taxable income often spikes in Q4. Planning ahead can create real savings.

- Ask to delay bonuses to next year if you're at peak income.
- Exercise options in January to delay potential capital gains into next tax year.
- "Bunch" charitable giving in alternating years to surpass standard deduction.

Case Study 3: Multi-Year Tax Strategy

Ravi, a regional CEO, faced overlapping Restricted Stock Unit (RSU) vests, bonus payouts, and deferred comp distributions—all within twenty-four months.

Here's what we did:

- Shifted future RSUs into 10b5-1 sales.
- Created a charitable plan to offset the first year.
- Delayed other income into retirement year + moved to Florida.
- Coordinated with CPA to harvest $90K in losses.

Over three years, Ravi reduced his effective tax rate by 8% and preserved over $400K in after-tax wealth.

Annual Executive Tax Planning Checklist

Time of Year	Action Item
January-March	- Run AMT projections for ISOs - Review RSU vesting schedule - Update DAF or charitable giving plans - Confirm deferral elections made prior year

Time of Year	Action Item
April–June	- Meet with CPA and advisor to project year's taxable income - Explore charitable bunching or gifting opportunities - Review state residency/tax implications
July–September	- Execute tax-loss harvesting if market is down - Review 10b5-1 plans for Q4 - Update estate planning for charitable legacy
October–December	- Finalize charitable contributions - Last call to defer discretionary income - Begin year-end equity exercise/sale coordination - Make Q4 estimated tax payments

Tax Planning Calendar for You

JANUARY

- Plan Incentive Stock Option exercises for early-year flexibility.
- Reassess 10b5-1 plans.
- Review Restricted Stock Unit vesting.

MARCH 15/APRIL 15

- Review final deadline for prior-year contributions to Donor-Advised Fund.
- File extensions if needed.

JUNE

- Examine midyear income projection with CPA.
- Estimate upcoming distributions.

SEPTEMBER

- Execute loss harvesting.
- Prep equity comp for Q4 events.

DECEMBER 31

- Last chance to donate stock, defer income, or adjust Restricted Stock Unit strategy.
- Make Roth conversions, Alternative Minimum Tax adjustments, and final tax decisions.

Final Thoughts: Planning = Return

Taxes are one of the only areas where proactive planning generates a guaranteed return. Every dollar you save in tax is a dollar you keep. When you combine equity compensation, bonuses, capital gains, and charitable giving, the opportunity to engineer a smarter tax outcome is massive.

And what about David, our panicked Incentive Stock Option friend of a client? With proper coordination, he took this strategy:

- Used Alternative Minimum Tax credit carryforwards over three years.
- Transitioned to a 10b5-1 plan.
- Funded a Donor-Advised Fund to manage future charitable gifts.
- Diversified and de-risked his equity exposure.

What began with panic ended with clarity—and a better financial life.

In the next chapter, we'll turn to investing—specifically, how to design a portfolio when your career and net worth are already heavily tied to your employer.

4

DON'T DOUBLE DOWN: SMARTER INVESTING FOR EXECUTIVES

LINDA HAD DEDICATED EIGHTEEN YEARS TO a pharmaceutical company, rising through the ranks to the senior leadership team. Her loyalty was evident not only in her tenure, but also in her portfolio—85% of her liquid net worth was tied up in company stock.

When an unexpected regulatory ruling cut the company's market cap by 50%, her net worth plummeted. Her career and her financial future had both been staked on the same outcome.

This is the harsh reality for many executives. While investing is often framed in terms of risk tolerance and market returns, executives must also consider employment-based exposure—where both your income and assets are tied to a single company. That's not just a concentration risk. It's a double bet.

The Executive Concentration Dilemma

You may often accumulate company exposure in these ways:

- Restricted Stock Units (RSUs) that vest annually and automatically add to stock holdings
- Options you hesitate to exercise, fearing regret or tax consequences
- Employee Stock Purchase Plan (ESPP) shares accumulated at a discount but rarely reviewed
- Bonuses tied to company performance
- Deferred compensation plans tied to company solvency

Add in personal loyalty, social pressure, and hope for future growth, and it's easy to see why many executives carry outsized positions in a single stock.

The psychological attachment to company stock is powerful. It symbolizes your contribution, loyalty, and the belief in your employer's success. But this same emotional connection can blind even seasoned professionals to real financial risks.

In one conversation, a COO told me, "Selling stock feels like betting against myself. It feels disloyal." But when we modeled her portfolio performance in down-market scenarios, she quickly saw the stakes: even a 25% drop in her company's stock would wipe out more wealth than five years of maxing out her 401(k) would build.

Step 1: Calculate Your Real Exposure

The first step toward risk management is awareness. Begin by calculating how much of your net worth is directly or indirectly tied to your employer. This includes

- Vested and unvested RSUs
- Unexercised stock options
- Deferred comp linked to company stock or solvency
- ESPP shares
- Retirement accounts holding company stock

Guideline: Limit total exposure to any single stock—especially your employer's—to no more than 10 to 15% of your net worth. Anything more significantly raises the risk of financial impairment.

Over time, unintentional overconcentration creeps in. Stock awards accumulate. Dividends are reinvested. Deferred compensation distributions default into employer stock. And before long, you're leveraged without realizing it.

We often recommend a full executive exposure audit where we map all equity grants, ownership, and expected future income sources tied to employer performance. This snapshot helps reset expectations and build a de-risking road map.

Step 2: Diversify Intelligently

You may hesitate to diversify due to capital gains taxes or fears of appearing disloyal. But inaction can be far more costly. The volatility of individual companies can drastically shift your financial trajectory overnight. Just ask the thousands of former employees of companies like Enron, GE, or Silicon Valley Bank.

Five Smart Strategies for Diversification

1. **Systematic Selling with a 10b5-1 Plan**

- SEC-approved plan to sell company stock on a preset schedule
- Reduces emotion, complies with insider trading laws, smooths tax impact

These plans are especially useful during blackout periods and can be modified annually. They provide legal insulation and discipline in uncertain markets.

2. **Charitable Gifting**

- Donate appreciated shares to a Donor-Advised Fund (DAF)
- Avoid capital gains, generate charitable deduction, support causes you care about

For high-income years, DAF contributions can help offset income from RSUs or option exercises.

3. **Exchange Funds**

- Pool company stock with other investors to achieve diversification without triggering taxes
- Ideal for large, concentrated positions ($1M+)

They allow you to trade a single stock position for a diversified portfolio of other stocks in a tax-deferred structure.

4. Hedging Strategies

- Use options-based tools to reduce downside risk
- Examples: collars, prepaid variable forwards, protective puts

These tools are best used with experienced financial and legal advisors to tailor contracts to specific exposure and liquidity goals.

5. Tax-Loss Harvesting and Gain Deferral

- Offset gains from company stock sales with harvested losses elsewhere
- Time gains across years to avoid bracket spikes

Timing matters. Selling after January 1 versus December 31 can have significant tax differences if you're navigating RSU vests, bonuses, or capital gain thresholds.

Case Study: The Path to Diversification

Erin, a senior leader at a Fortune 100 consumer products firm, had $3.2M in company stock and had never sold a single share. Over time, she'd built an unintentional bet on one outcome.

We created a three-year road map to diversify her holdings:

- Sell $250K/year via a 10b5-1 plan.
- Gift $100K of low-basis shares to a Donor-Advised Fund.
- Exercise Incentive Stock Options gradually to avoid Alternative Minimum Tax spikes.
- Use proceeds to build a diversified core-satellite portfolio.

We also incorporated a real estate fund to provide passive income and a private credit allocation for consistent yield in low-rate environments. Her charitable goals became a part of her long-term legacy strategy through the Donor-Advised Fund.

By year three, she had reduced her employer stock exposure from 78% to 24%, without triggering massive taxes in a single year. She remained fully committed to her employer, but her personal net worth was now insulated from company-specific shocks.

Step 3: Build a Resilient Portfolio

A resilient portfolio starts with a clear investment policy. We use a core-satellite approach, combining broad market exposure (the core) with targeted investments (satellites) for growth, income, or diversification.

Core Elements

- Global equity Exchange-Traded Funds
- Intermediate-duration bonds
- Cash reserves or ultra-short-term bonds

Satellite Components

- Private equity and venture capital
- Private real estate
- Hedge funds

We also build asset location strategies—placing tax-inefficient assets (like bonds or Real Estate Investment Trusts called REITs) in tax-deferred accounts, and tax-efficient investments in taxable accounts.

Step 4: Incorporate Alternatives for Strategic Diversification

Alternative investments can help executives further diversify beyond the traditional 60/40 portfolio. Used properly, you introduce new sources of return and reduce correlation to public markets.

Private Equity (PE)

- Invest in non-public companies with long-term growth potential
- Lock-up periods: seven to ten years
- Higher return potential, higher illiquidity risk

Best For: Those with surplus capital and long time horizons

Venture Capital (VC)

- High-risk, high-reward investments in startups
- Illiquid and volatile, but can yield exponential returns

Best For: Tech-savvy executives seeking exposure to innovation (limit to <5% of portfolio)

Hedge Funds

- Employ long-short, macro, arbitrage, and other complex strategies
- Lower correlation to equity markets; potential for downside protection

Best For: Diversifying public equity exposure; requires due diligence and manager access

Private Real Estate

- Income-producing properties or real estate funds
- Offers tangible asset exposure, depreciation benefits, and inflation hedging

Best For: Income generation and portfolio stability

Private Credit

- Lending to private companies in exchange for yield
- Higher returns than bonds, but with more risk

Best For: Those needing passive income in a low-yield environment

Behavioral Considerations: The Emotional Weight of Selling

Selling company stock feels different:

- It may feel disloyal.
- It may be misinterpreted by peers or management.
- It can feel like giving up on the upside.

But diversification is a discipline, not a disavowal. Loyalty is demonstrated in your leadership—not your brokerage account. Protecting your wealth allows you to continue contributing at your highest level without unnecessary financial stress.

One executive likened it to creating "a financial firewall" between her career and her family's future.

Step 5: Manage Liquidity and Flexibility

You may often experience a liquidity mismatch: high net worth, low cash flow.

Solutions

- Maintain six to twelve months of expenses in cash or equivalents.
- Use planned liquidation of Restricted Stock Units or exercised options to meet upcoming obligations.
- Consider securities-backed lines of credit (SBLOCs) with caution.
- Build a portfolio ladder of short-term investments for strategic withdrawals.

This flexibility allows you to weather market downturns, tax events, or career transitions without needing to tap into company stock under pressure.

Final Thoughts

When you're an executive, your job is already a bet, as your compensation and net worth are significantly tied to the performance of your company's stock. Your portfolio doesn't need to be another risk. Overconcentration is a silent risk that often grows unnoticed until it's too late. But with a clear plan, diversification strategy, and disciplined execution, you can turn your company-provided wealth into a secure and flexible future.

Linda learned this lesson the hard way by losing wealth when her company had a downturn. Erin learned it in time and diversified.

The goal is for you to learn it proactively so you can enjoy both your career and your wealth with confidence.

In the next chapter, we'll explore how to protect everything you've built through smart estate planning and multigenerational wealth strategies.

5

LEGACY PLANNING THAT WON'T BORE YOU TO DEATH

RACHEL, A PHARMACEUTICAL EXECUTIVE, NEVER IMAGINED she'd face a life-threatening illness so suddenly. She was only fifty-six. With two adult children, one with special needs, her $12 million in assets, and a demanding career, estate planning had always felt like a "do this later" task. But with time now uncertain, she was faced with urgent decisions—none of which had been addressed in writing. There was no will, no trust, and no strategy for transferring the wealth she had worked a lifetime to build.

Rachel's story, though dramatic, is not rare.

You yourself may be so hyper-focused on career and accumulating wealth that you have delayed planning for what happens next. But estate planning is not just about death—it's about control, clarity, and legacy.

In Rachel's case, the absence of planning led to weeks of legal wrangling, court petitions for guardianship over her special needs son, and emotional strain on her family during an already difficult time.

Why You Must Think Differently

Estate planning is essential for everyone, but executives face even more unique challenges such as these:

- Complex compensation structures with illiquid or delayed-pay assets
- Exposure to both federal and state estate taxes
- Retirement plans and deferred compensation with strict transfer rules
- Privacy and reputational risk if estates go through public probate

- Higher likelihood of philanthropic intent and multigenerational planning

You are often advised to build wealth. Far fewer of us are advised on how to protect and pass the wealth down. This chapter explores how to create a plan that reflects not only your assets but your values—and ensures your legacy is intentional, not accidental.

Step 1: Get the Essentials in Place

Every executive, regardless of age or wealth, should start with these foundational documents:

- Last Will and Testament: Directs asset distribution and appoints guardians for minor children
- Durable Power of Attorney: Allows someone to manage your finances if you become incapacitated
- Health Care Proxy and Living Will: Names someone to make medical decisions when you cannot and outlines your end-of-life preferences

Without these, decisions about your health and wealth could be made by a court-appointed stranger.

Scenario: No Will, Big Problems

Jonathan, a forty-eight-year-old tech executive, died unexpectedly with $7 million in assets but no estate documents. His divorced spouse contested the estate. Probate took eighteen months, assets were frozen, and legal fees exceeded $300,000.

Lesson: Even a basic estate plan could have preserved family harmony, protected privacy, and saved significant costs.

Step 2: Use Trusts to Increase Control and Efficiency

Trusts aren't just for the ultra-wealthy. They are tools to avoid probate, streamline distribution, reduce taxes, and ensure privacy.

Revocable Living Trust

- Avoids probate
- Keeps affairs private
- Can be amended or revoked during your lifetime

Irrevocable Trusts

- Used for tax reduction, asset protection, and legacy planning
- Removes assets from your taxable estate
- Often used to hold life insurance, business shares, or investment accounts

Scenario: Rachel's Trusts

Initially, Rachel established a revocable trust to hold her brokerage accounts and Restricted Stock Units. Later, she created an Irrevocable Life Insurance Trust (ILIT) for her $3 million policy. This move kept her insurance proceeds out of her estate and ensured her heirs received the funds quickly and tax-free.

Step 3: Address Non-Probate Assets

Many assets transfer outside your will or trust:

- Retirement accounts (401(k), IRA): Governed by beneficiary designations
- Life insurance: Proceeds go directly to listed beneficiaries

- Deferred compensation: Subject to company plan rules
- POD (Payable on Death) and TOD (Transfer on Death) accounts: Transfer directly to named individuals

Key Tip: Review these designations regularly—especially after life events like marriage, divorce, or the birth of a child.

Scenario: Beneficiary Oversight

Maria had remarried but forgot to update her IRA beneficiary. When she passed, her ex-husband inherited $850,000—not her new spouse or children.

Step 4: Consider Lifetime Giving

Gifting during your lifetime can

- Reduce your taxable estate
- Help heirs when they need it most
- Allow you to witness your impact

Gifting Options

- Annual Exclusion Gifts: Up to $18,000 per person (2025)
- 529 Plans: Front-load five years of gifts for education
- Grantor Retained Annuity Trusts (GRATs): Shift appreciating assets with minimal gift tax
- Charitable Giving
    - Donor-Advised Funds (DAF)
    - Charitable Remainder Trusts (CRT)
    - Family Foundations

Case Study: Living Philanthropy

Jeff and Elena, two biotech executives, contributed $100,000/year to a DAF to teach their children about giving. They let their kids choose which causes to support, blending tax strategy with family values.

Step 5: Plan for Business and Equity Compensation

You face added complexity from

- Nontransferable stock options and restricted RSUs
- Deferred comp with strict timing and ownership rules
- Ownership in private businesses

Coordinate your plan with HR, legal, and financial professionals. Consider

- Liquidity planning for estate tax payments
- Buy-sell agreements for business interests
- Trusts tailored to hold and protect illiquid or complex assets

Scenario: Equity Without Liquidity

A founder of a private firm passed unexpectedly. His 45% ownership stake couldn't be sold quickly. The family had to borrow funds to pay estate taxes, then sell under pressure at a discount to what the real value of the company was in order to become liquid.

Step 6: Talk to Your Heirs

The best estate plans include a conversation. Transparency builds trust and reduces tension.

Benefits of Family Discussions

- Set expectations
- Reduce surprises and legal disputes
- Reinforce values and stewardship

Tip: Host a family meeting with your spouse, adult children, and key advisors. Consider sharing a summary (not all dollar amounts) of your plan.

Step 7: Review Regularly

Life evolves—so should your plan. Review it every three to five years or when major life events occur:

- Marriage, divorce, or remarriage
- Death of a spouse
- Promotion at current company
- Changing employer
- Birth of children or grandchildren
- Relocation to a different state
- Major asset changes (sale of business, inheritance, for example)

Estate law is also fluid. Tax exemptions change, state laws update, and strategies evolve. Make sure your plan still fits your life.

Final Thoughts

Rachel passed away three years after her diagnosis but with peace of mind. Her estate plan provided clarity, avoided family conflict, and ensured her legacy lived on in the way she intended.

For executives, estate planning is not a luxury. It is a leadership act. It turns your hard work into lasting impact. It ensures your wealth is a blessing, not a burden, for the people you love.

Your estate plan is not just a legal document. It is a reflection of your values, your voice, and your vision.

In the next chapter, we'll explore how to coordinate your advisory team and build a family office structure—even without nine-figure wealth.

6

BUILDING YOUR FAMILY OFFICE (WITHOUT NEEDING $500M)

TOM AND MICHELLE WERE THE TYPICAL power couple—she a partner at a prestigious law firm, he a senior executive at a global tech company. Their combined income exceeded $1.5 million annually, and their net worth hovered around $12 million.

On paper, they were living the dream. But beneath the surface, their financial life was a tangled web of spreadsheets, advisors, and unanswered questions.

Here's their tangled financial picture:

- Four separate financial advisors managing different accounts
- An estate plan written before their second child was born
- A CPA who filed their taxes but didn't coordinate with their financial people
- A deferred compensation plan with a looming distribution
- A rental property business with no succession plan

Tom finally admitted, "It feels like we're the CEOs of a company with no CFO."

What they needed wasn't another advisor. They needed a structure. A system. A family office.

What Is a Family Office?

A traditional family office is a privately held company that manages investments, taxes, estate planning, philanthropy, and administrative functions for a wealthy family. It typically requires $100M+ to justify the cost. These structures employ a full-time team of professionals—chief investment officers, tax experts, attorneys, philanthropic consultants—all aligned to execute a single family's long-term plan.

But executives like Tom and Michelle don't need nine figures to benefit from a similar model. Instead, I help clients implement what my firm and I call the Efficient Family Office℠—a coordinated, centralized approach to managing wealth using the principles laid out by Michael McDermott in his book *The Efficient Family Office: Why You Should (and Can) Build Your Own Financial Dream Team Like the World's Wealthiest Families.*

This model captures the core benefits of a traditional family office—alignment, integration, and strategy—without the cost or complexity. It enables affluent families to run their financial lives with the same clarity and coordination you bring to your businesses. It's not about having more money—it's about managing what you have with more intention.

Why You Need a Centralized Model

The modern executive has

- Multiple income sources (salary, bonus, equity, real estate, private investments),
- Complex tax planning needs,
- Estate planning considerations for minor children, aging parents, or blended families,
- Charitable giving goals, and
- A lack of time to manage it all.

The Efficient Family Office brings these pieces together under one unified umbrella. Such structure helps our clients

- Make smarter, more integrated decisions,
- Coordinate professionals and avoid duplication or gaps,

- Gain clarity and confidence in their entire financial picture, and
- Delegate lower-impact decisions to trusted professionals.

Step 1: Assemble the Right Team

Your core team should include the following professionals:

- Financial advisor to create portfolio design, equity comp management, financial independence modeling, savings strategies, and withdrawal strategies
- CPA to handle tax projections, Alternative Minimum Tax mitigation, multi-state planning, income deferral optimization
- Estate attorney to draft and update wills, revocable and irrevocable trusts, guardianship, succession plans
- Insurance professional to assess risk management across life, disability, umbrella, liability, property and casualty policies
- Philanthropic consultant or Donor-Advised Fund administrator to suggest and handle strategic giving and family involvement

But beyond having these roles, it's essential all the players collaborate. Too often, professionals work in silos. The Efficient Family Office encourages the team to meet annually to align strategies, that they all share dashboards and secure document storage, and that there is centralized project management and note tracking.

Your financial advisor should act as the "quarterback," ensuring each team member is aligned with your family's mission and communicating proactively.

Step 2: Build Your System

An Efficient Family Office includes a secure, organized way to view and manage your financial life. We help clients implement tools such as these, and you will want to follow a similar plan:

- A dynamic net worth dashboard with real-time updates across all bank, investment, and loan accounts
- A cloud-based document vault for wills, trusts, powers of attorney, tax returns, insurance policies, and employment agreements
- An annual financial calendar outlining key planning dates—Restricted Stock Unit vests, tax filing deadlines, option expiration, insurance reviews, charitable contribution targets
- Key performance indicator tracking for goals like annual giving, savings rates, and legacy milestones

This infrastructure allows families to manage complexity without drowning in it. It's about turning chaos into calm.

Step 3: Delegate Strategically

High-performing executives often have trouble letting go. They're used to being in control, but financial decision fatigue is real, and it steals time from your family, work, and personal life.

We help clients create a delegation framework, and here's what that looks like:

- Tier 1: Executive oversight: tax returns, estate drafts, major investment changes
- Tier 2: Advisor execution with executive approval: Restricted Stock Unit sales, 10b5-1 adjustments, portfolio rebalancing

- Tier 3: Fully delegated: tax-loss harvesting, Donor-Advised Fund distributions, financial reporting, charitable administration

Delegation doesn't mean giving up control. It means leveraging experts so you can focus on the decisions that matter most.

Case Study: Building a Delegation Structure

Steve, a biotech executive, was managing his family's finances through a combination of spreadsheets and late-night email chains with financial people, accountants, and charities. We helped him streamline the work:

- Shift day-to-day financial execution to his advisory team
- Set up a quarterly report card showing progress toward family goals
- Implement automated charitable giving through a Donor-Advised Fund
- Establish a secure vault and shared portal for tax and legal documents

Within three months, Steve was spending 80% less time on administrative tasks and had full visibility into everything.

Step 4: Plan Like a Business

Think of your family like a values-driven enterprise. You have objectives, assets, liabilities, key stakeholders, risk exposure, and long-term growth plans. The Efficient Family Office applies corporate strategy to personal wealth by

- Setting quarterly or semi-annual planning goals,

- Holding an annual review with the full team,
- Evaluating key performance indicators like tax drag, investment expenses, and savings rates,
- Revisiting mission statements for giving or wealth transfer, and
- Using rolling five- and ten-year financial projections for scenario modeling.

One of our clients created an internal "family balance sheet" and quarterly financial updates that their college-aged children reviewed together. It wasn't about disclosing every detail—it was about modeling stewardship and strategy.

Step 5: Prepare the Next Generation

True wealth is measured by impact, not just dollars. That's why families committed to the Efficient Family Office model also commit to raising the next generation of thoughtful stewards.

Here are some of the activities they do together:

- Host age-appropriate financial literacy sessions (like a money bootcamp)
- Invite children into giving decisions and impact reports
- Use stories, family history, and shared values to anchor planning
- Include heirs in advisor meetings, when appropriate, to build comfort

Case Study: Preparing a Legacy

Marissa and Daniel had three children in their teens and early twenties. We created a multigenerational planning structure that included these activities:

- A legacy letter documenting their life lessons, values, and hopes for future generations
- Quarterly family meetings with a rotating facilitator among the children
- Age-based trust distributions tied to milestones and financial education

The transformation wasn't just financial—it was cultural. The children began to see wealth not as entitlement, but as opportunity and responsibility.

Step 6: Selecting and Vetting Your Advisors

With a sophisticated structure comes a need for highly qualified professionals. Here's what to look for and how to select and vet yours:

- Credentials and specialization: CFP®, CPWA®, CPA, JD, CLU, CFA. While a few letters after someone's name cannot guarantee they are knowledgeable, this shows the professional's desire to learn and become better at their craft.
- Specialization in executive and high-net-worth planning
- Proven experience with equity compensation, multigenerational planning, and tax and estate strategies
- Transparent fee structures
- Willingness to collaborate with other professionals

Questions to ask:

- Are you a fiduciary?
- How do you coordinate with my other advisors?
- What's your experience with clients like me?
- Do you have a network of specialists you bring in?
- Can you show me real examples of your planning work?

Watch for these red flags:

- Commission-based compensation models with vague incentives
- Not a fiduciary
- One-size-fits-all financial plans
- Lack of familiarity with Restricted Stock Units, Incentive Stock Options, or deferred comp
- No formal client service calendar or proactive outreach

You are hiring department heads for your family's enterprise—treat the task like a key executive search.

Final Case Study: The Transformation

Tom and Michelle implemented our Efficient Family Office over twelve months. Here are some of their results:

- Consolidated six accounts into two coordinated advisory relationships
- Developed a rolling ten-year tax and estate strategy
- Hosted their first family wealth retreat and legacy planning session
- Delegated operational tasks and refocused on strategic decisions
- Created a structured charitable strategy tied to alma maters and causes

Most importantly, they felt aligned for the first time in years. What had once felt like a burden became a point of pride.

Final Thoughts

You don't need to be a billionaire to benefit from a family office mindset. If your financial life feels complex, disorganized, or overwhelming, a coordinated model brings clarity.

The Efficient Family Office gives you more than better results—it gives you back your time, your peace of mind, and your power to lead your financial life with confidence. While my team and I take on most of the heavy lifting for our clients, you can create a similar structure for your family and be a steward of your wealth. Start with seeing if you have the right professionals on your team and then go from there.

7

WHEN YOUR CAREER CROSSES CONTINENTS

NINA HAD ALWAYS DREAMED OF WORKING abroad. As a rising star in her pharmaceutical company's leadership pipeline, she was offered a position in London with a generous expat package. Her husband was a dual US–French citizen, and their two teenagers were excited for the adventure. But while Nina was busy preparing for new colleagues and a different culture, her financial life was preparing for chaos.

Six months into the move, she was hit with an unexpected UK tax bill. Her US CPA had never worked with British filings. Her estate plan—perfectly fine in Pennsylvania—was now nearly useless. To top it off, a foreign bank account she opened triggered a reporting requirement she didn't know existed. She wasn't in trouble. Not yet. But she was far from in control.

Nina's story isn't rare. Today's executives are more mobile, international, and globally compensated than ever before. But most are unprepared for the complexity that follows them across borders.

This chapter is about helping you build clarity and confidence if your career—or retirement—takes you global.

Step 1: Understand Your Tax Residency

The most important—and often most confusing—concept for international executives is tax residency. Different countries use different tests to determine whether you owe taxes.

In the US, tax residency is straightforward:

- US citizens and green card holders are taxed on worldwide income, regardless of where they live.

- Even if you live abroad, the IRS still expects a tax return—and compliance with foreign income reporting rules.

Other countries often use these tests:

- Days-based tests (for example, in the UK and Canada): You're considered a resident if you're physically present for a certain number of days.
- Ties-based tests: Evaluating where you have a home, work, family, or financial interests.

Planning Tips

- Use the Foreign Earned Income Exclusion (FEIE) if eligible ($126,500 per person in 2024).
- Claim Foreign Tax Credits (FTCs) to avoid double taxation.
- Track travel days meticulously—this can make or break your tax status in multiple countries.

Step 2: Coordinate Cross-Border Tax Planning

The US has tax treaties with dozens of countries, but you don't eliminate complexity. If you move abroad or work for foreign companies, you may face these tax situations:

- Double taxation if not careful with elections and credits
- Phantom income due to different treatment of deferred comp or stock options
- Currency risk and translation issues for earnings and expenses

Take the case of Javier, a dual citizen working in both Mexico and the US. His Incentive Stock Options were tax-advantaged in the US but fully taxable in Mexico at exercise. We helped him build a dual-timeline tax projection model to determine the optimal exercise strategy.

Planning Points

- Review how stock options, Restricted Stock Units, and Employee Stock Purchase Plans are taxed in both countries.
- Pre-exit tax planning is crucial—your departure date can define your tax year.
- Engage a cross-border tax advisor early—not after your first surprise bill.

Step 3: Prepare for International Reporting Obligations

US taxpayers with foreign financial assets have strict reporting rules. Failure to file can result in significant penalties—even if no tax is due.

Common reporting requirements include this alphabet soup of items:

- FBAR (FinCEN 114): Report foreign bank and financial accounts if total exceeds $10,000 at any point in the year.
- FATCA (Form 8938): Additional asset reporting is required for higher thresholds.
- Form 8621: Required for Passive Foreign Investment Companies (PFICs), which includes many foreign mutual funds.

One client opened a French investment account with a local advisor. It included a European mutual fund—classified as a PFIC. The compliance paperwork took more time than the investment earned.

Checklist

- Ask your international bank or advisor for a list of all reportable accounts.
- Avoid investing in non-US mutual funds if possible.
- Keep meticulous records of foreign income, account balances, and ownership percentages.

Step 4: Rebuild Your Estate Plan for Global Validity

An estate plan that works in New York might not mean anything in Singapore.

Global executives must account for these tax implications:

- Differing inheritance laws (some countries use forced heirship rules)
- Local probate systems (which can be slow, expensive, and public)
- Multiple jurisdictions for assets (real estate, bank accounts, pensions)

We helped one couple living in Zurich revise their US revocable trust, add Swiss powers of attorney, and create a separate will for their overseas property. Without that plan, their heirs would have faced years of legal confusion.

Best Practices

- Coordinate your US estate attorney with an advisor licensed in your country of residence.
- Update powers of attorney and healthcare directives to be valid where you live.
- Consider separate wills for assets in different countries.

Step 5: Clarify Your Retirement Abroad Strategy

You may dream of retiring abroad—spending your golden years in Italy, Portugal, or Costa Rica. But this decision impacts

- Healthcare access and insurance coverage,
- Tax treatment of retirement income,
- Cost-of-living and inflation exposure, and
- Estate and gift tax rules.

Before making the leap, do this:

- Run a comparative cost-of-living analysis.
- Understand whether your Social Security and pension income will be taxed locally.
- Review how your Medicare benefits may or may not apply overseas.

One client, Matt, retired to Portugal at sixty. His US-based IRA distributions were taxed both in the US and partially in Portugal until we helped him use the tax treaty to reduce the effective rate and structured his withdrawals accordingly.

Tool: Expat Retirement Readiness Checklist

- Confirm tax treaty benefits with destination country.
- Analyze healthcare costs and coverage options.
- Set up a local financial team (accountant, attorney, and other advisors).
- Build an international banking and cash flow strategy.
- Review estate plan for cross-border enforceability.

Step 6: Navigate Currency and Investment Diversification

Managing wealth across currencies introduces new risks—and new opportunities.

You may earn in dollars, spend in euros, and invest globally. That requires

- Currency hedging strategies,
- Tax-aware international investing, and
- Diversification to protect against geopolitical and regulatory risks.

One executive living in Singapore held over 70% of her net worth in US equities. We restructured her portfolio to include

- Developed and emerging market funds,
- Hard-asset real estate in the region, and
- A partial cash hedge in local currency.

Pro Tip: Avoid currency conversion whiplash. Anchor your financial plan in your spending currency (where you'll use the money) and adjust your investment strategy accordingly.

Step 7: Leverage Global Giving and Philanthropy

If you're charitably inclined, international giving introduces both opportunities and restrictions.

The US tax code only allows deductions for donations to US-based 501(c)(3) charities, so donating directly to a foreign nonprofit might not be deductible.

But you can do this:

- Use a US-based Donor-Advised Fund to grant money to international partners via equivalency determinations.
- Establish a dual-qualified charity if you're involved in large-scale giving across borders.
- Incorporate charitable goals into your estate and legacy plan globally.

I worked with an executive living in the UK to support children's education in India. By routing gifts through a DAF with global reach, we ensured both impact and tax efficiency.

Step 8: Engage Your Family in the Global Journey

Living, working, or retiring abroad affects your entire family—logistically, emotionally, and financially.

We recommend

- Hosting regular family meetings to align on location, schools, housing, healthcare
- Using the global move as a platform for teaching financial literacy
- Involving children in charitable projects and legacy planning
- Preparing adult children for international inheritance or trust structures

One family created a "global values charter" during their time living in Japan. Each year, they reviewed their philanthropic goals and updated their travel and giving plans around shared values.

Case Study: The Global Blueprint

Nina and her husband ultimately spent five years in the UK, then relocated to Lisbon for retirement. Here's how their financial blueprint evolved:

- Coordinated with a cross-border tax firm for dual filings
- Created dual estate plans valid in the US and Portugal
- Converted company equity into a diversified global portfolio
- Moved their giving to an international Donor-Advised Fund
- Added Portuguese healthcare and long-term care options

Today, Nina says, "We're not just living abroad—we're living aligned."

Final Thoughts

In a world of increasing mobility and opportunity, wealth management can no longer be purely domestic. Whether you're working across borders, managing foreign assets, or retiring internationally, your financial life needs a global lens.

That doesn't mean complexity has to overwhelm you. With the right team, systems, and planning, you can turn international uncertainty into clarity—and opportunity.

Remember: The true executive edge isn't just success at home. It's knowing how to carry your values, vision, and strategy anywhere in the world.

In the next chapter, we'll explore this question: What happens when you no longer need to work? How do you make the leap from success to significance no matter where you retire? From obligation to freedom?

8

FIRE THE ALARM CLOCK: YOU'RE FINANCIALLY FREE

CARLOS HAD SPENT TWENTY-TWO YEARS CLIMBING the corporate ladder. As a C-suite executive at a global consumer brand, he had achieved professional success, accumulated substantial wealth, and built a reputation as a thoughtful leader. But as he approached his fifties, something began to shift. The drive that once fueled him now felt like inertia. He wasn't ready to retire, but he also didn't want to keep sprinting.

"I want to know when I can step away on my terms," he told me. "Not just financially, but mentally and emotionally. What does that even look like?"

This chapter is about answering that very question. For executives, the idea of retirement is often less appealing than the idea of freedom—the ability to choose how you spend your time without financial constraint. We call this point "work optional."

What Does "Work Optional" Really Mean?

It's not just about hitting a number. It's about creating a life where work is a choice, not a necessity. That could mean

- Starting a nonprofit
- Teaching at a university
- Consulting part-time
- Traveling extensively
- Focusing on family or health

The key is knowing that you have the financial flexibility to make those choices confidently. And just as importantly, that you've prepared mentally, emotionally, and logistically to embrace a new lifestyle that may be very different from your working years.

Step 1: Define Your Personal Vision

Start by asking yourself these questions:

- What excites me outside of work?
- What legacy do I want to leave?
- What does a fulfilling next chapter look like?
- How do I want to structure my days and weeks?

Carlos realized he wanted to focus on mentorship, travel with his wife, and serving on a few nonprofit boards. Once that was clear, the financial planning became more focused—and more meaningful. Without this clarity, even the most robust balance sheet can feel empty.

To help clients visualize this transition, my colleagues and I often use a life design matrix:

- Core identity: What do I value most?
- Purpose: How do I want to contribute?
- Joy: What activities or experiences give me energy?
- Structure: How will I create rhythm and routine?

Your answers to these question shape your financial decisions, goals, and timeline.

Step 2: Calculate Your "Enough" Number

Most executives ask, "How much do I need to retire?" But the better question is, "What lifestyle do I want, and what does that cost?"

To determine your "enough" number, consider these numbers first:

- Annual living expenses (now and future)
- Healthcare costs (pre-Medicare and after)
- One-time expenses (such as travel, weddings, home projects)
- Tax obligations (including capital gains, Roth conversions, Required Minimum Distributions from retirement accounts, usually after age seventy-three)
- Inflation and cost-of-living increases
- Legacy goals (gifting, estate planning, charitable giving)

We use detailed cash flow modeling, stress testing, and Monte Carlo simulations to analyze these numbers:

- Safe withdrawal rates (typically 3 to 4% annually)
- Market volatility impact
- Asset longevity under various spending levels
- Tax-efficient drawdown strategies

If your desired lifestyle costs $250,000 per year, you likely need $6 to $8 million in liquid, investable assets. But that number changes based on income sources (for example, you may have rental income or deferred comp), location, health, and goals.

Step 3: Assess Your Healthcare Bridge

For executives retiring before age sixty-five, healthcare becomes a major planning point. Medicare eligibility starts at sixty-five, but if you retire at fifty-five, you need a bridge strategy.

You have these options:

- COBRA: Temporary continuation of your employer's plan (between to eighteen to thirty-six months)

- ACA Marketplace plans: Often viable, especially with income-based subsidies
- Spousal coverage: If your spouse continues to work, consider joining that plan
- Private insurance: For those desiring specialized or concierge-level care

We helped Carlos evaluate

- A COBRA extension for eighteen months, followed by an ACA plan
- Prefunding a Health Savings Account (HSA) before leaving work
- Budgeting $25,000/year for healthcare costs, adjusted for inflation

This ensured there were no gaps—and no surprises—in coverage during early retirement.

Step 4: Take the Work-Optional Readiness Quiz

We've developed a proprietary readiness assessment that evaluates more than just net worth. Rate yourself on a scale of 1 to 5, with 1 meaning the "no" and 5 meaning "definitely", in the following areas:

Lifestyle Readiness

- I know how I want to spend my time in retirement.
- I have hobbies, interests, or relationships outside of work.
- I'm excited, not anxious, about a more flexible schedule.

Psychological Readiness

- I am comfortable with the idea of no longer receiving a paycheck.
- My identity is not solely tied to my job title or employer.

- I can see myself saying "no" to opportunities that don't align with my purpose.

Financial Readiness

- I've built a financial plan that includes healthcare, taxes, and long-term care.
- I have a distribution strategy in place.
- My spouse or partner is aligned with our financial and lifestyle goals.

Score

- 36–45: Ready to transition
- 26–35: Almost there—refine your plan
- Under 25: Focus on clarity, purpose, and structure before making a change

Step 5: Model Multiple Scenarios

We encourage clients to build flexible plans that include these aspects of retirement:

- A sabbatical or "trial retirement"
- Phased exit (reduced hours or responsibilities)
- Consulting or board work
- A second act (that could be entrepreneurship, writing, or coaching)

Use these scenarios to evaluate

- Longevity of your assets,
- Cash flow timing and liquidity needs,
- Potential changes in tax brackets, and
- The impact of Social Security claiming strategies.

Carlos tested five variations:

1. Full retirement at fifty-five with no income
2. Part-time consulting for five years
3. Relocating to a state with no income tax
4. Increased travel and charitable giving
5. A health scare requiring additional care and expenses

Modeling these scenarios helped him see the trade-offs—and avoid unnecessary fear.

Step 6: Transition from Accumulation to Distribution

This is where mindset and mechanics converge. You're no longer just saving—you're spending, reallocating, and preserving.

Key considerations

- Convert concentrated stock positions into diversified holdings.
- Sequence withdrawals for tax efficiency (one example: brokerage → IRA → Roth).
- Use Roth conversions to manage RMDs and create tax-free income.
- Maintain cash reserves of one to two years of expenses.
- Review asset allocation for income stability and longevity.

We helped Carlos build a "bucketing" strategy that looked like this:

- Bucket 1: Two years of cash and short-term bonds
- Bucket 2: Three to seven years of moderate-risk income investments

- Bucket 3: Long-term growth assets (stocks, real estate, private equity)

This allowed him to spend confidently without selling during downturns.

Step 7: Redefine Your Identity and Purpose

Stepping away from a demanding career can create a vacuum. To fill it intentionally, I often suggest my clients consider some of these activities:

- Journaling or vision boarding your ideal day, week, and year
- Volunteering or mentoring before you leave your role
- Creating a purpose portfolio: meaningful projects, relationships, and learning goals
- Replacing "What do you do?" with "What are you exploring right now?"

Carlos initially struggled. But after three months of travel, he found joy in mentoring MBA students at a local university, writing for industry publications, and hosting leadership roundtables.

Step 8: Communicate with Your Partner and Family

One of the most overlooked parts of retirement planning is communication. Here are some recommendations:

- A shared vision exercise with your spouse or partner, discussing what you want retirement to look like and how you want to spend your time

- Family meetings to discuss financial changes, estate plans, and legacy goals
- Honest conversations about new roles and responsibilities at home and how things can change as both spouses are at home and around one another all day

Step 9: Prepare for the Emotional Curve

You may experience a post-career transition curve, and you may cycle through all these emotions:

1. Euphoria: "I'm free!"
2. Ambiguity: "Now what?"
3. Exploration: "What's next?"
4. Integration: "I've found my rhythm."

Having a coach, therapist, or peer network can ease this transition. I have found that men especially struggle with this transition and recommend they find something to "retire into and not just out of."

Case Study: The Slow Exit

Carlos negotiated a phased transition over eighteen months:

- He moved to a four-day workweek and joined a bowling league on Fridays.
- Began consulting with two startups on the side. He connected with the local Chamber of Commerce for connections.
- Created a five-year philanthropic giving plan.
- Took a two-month sabbatical with his wife in Europe.

He eventually stepped away fully, with clarity and confidence. Today, he mentors MBA students, sits on two nonprofit boards, and says, "You're right, I feel like I've retired *into* something—not *away* from something."

Final Thoughts

Making work optional is about designing your next chapter. It's not about retiring from something—it's about moving toward something better. Financial freedom is only meaningful when it's aligned with your values, your passions, and your relationships.

You've spent decades building success. Now it's time to define significance. In the next chapter, we'll explore how to turn wealth into impact—how to use your resources not just for freedom, but for purpose.

9

FROM SUCCESS TO SIGNIFICANCE

JENNIFER RETIRED EARLY. SHE HAD BUILT an impressive portfolio, totaling over $15 million. Her financial plan was airtight. Her estate was in order. Her tax strategy was efficient. But three months into retirement, she admitted something was off.

"I thought I'd feel free," she said. "Instead, I feel aimless."

Jennifer's story is common. For many executives, wealth has been the measure of progress. But at a certain point, accumulating more stops adding value. What matters next isn't how much you have, it's how well you use it.

This chapter is about transforming wealth from a source of security to a source of significance.

Step 1: Reconnect with What Matters

Purpose isn't something you stumble into after retirement. It's cultivated intentionally through reflection, conversation, and exploration.

Self-Assessment: Purpose Discovery Quiz

Take this short quiz to reflect on your sense of purpose:

- Do I feel excited when I think about the next phase of my life?
- Can I name three causes or communities I feel passionate about?
- Have I envisioned what a fulfilling day or week in retirement looks like?
- Have I discussed these ideas with my partner or family?

If you answered "no" to more than one of these, it may be time to step back and spend time on purpose alignment.

Journal Prompt: What would I regret not doing with the time and wealth I've been given?

For Jennifer, purpose meant mentoring young women in STEM, funding scholarships, and writing a memoir for her grandchildren. For others, it may mean environmental activism, interfaith work, or rebuilding relationships.

Step 2: Align Wealth with Values

You've spent your career building wealth. Now it's time to deploy it with intention.

Impact Investing

Impact investing allows you to align your investment portfolio with your personal values.

Key options

- ESG Funds: Invest in companies with strong environmental, social, and governance practices.
- Thematic Exchange-Traded Funds (called ETFs): Target issues like clean energy, gender equity, or affordable housing.
- Private impact funds: Invest in social enterprises or community-based solutions.
- Direct investing: Engage in early-stage venture capital in fields you believe in.

Impact investing can yield both financial returns and social dividends. We helped one client transition $2 million of her portfolio into climate-forward funds and local community development bonds—preserving return targets while reflecting her environmental values.

Mission-Driven Philanthropy

Rather than sporadic donations, structure your giving for the longer term:

- Use a Donor-Advised Fund to front-load charitable contributions and grants over time.
- Establish a Charitable Remainder Trust for lifetime income and legacy giving.
- Set up a private foundation for family governance, ongoing involvement, and targeted causes.

Activity: Create a Values and Vision Grid.

- List the top three causes you care about.
- Consider the ideal impact (examples would be scholarships, clean water, job training).
- Earmark the amount of time/money you'd commit.

Then identify how your current wealth plan supports—or conflicts with—this vision.

Step 3: Include Your Family in the Mission

Your legacy extends beyond assets. The most powerful inheritance is a shared sense of values and purpose.

Here are some activities to engage family:

- Create a family mission statement. Gather input from each member, and articulate shared principles and goals.
- Hold annual giving meetings. Let each family member research and pitch a cause for funding.
- Convene storytelling dinners. Share stories of how the family's wealth was built and the sacrifices behind it.

- Play philanthropy as a game. For young children, allocate $500 in a "giving challenge" to choose where and how it's donated.

The Morgan family hosted a retreat each fall where they reviewed their Donor-Advised Fund grants, discussed community needs, and voted on next year's giving plan. It became their most cherished family tradition.

Step 4: Strategic Giving to Family and Charity

Giving to Family

Strategic family giving teaches stewardship:

- Annual exclusion gifts: Gift up to $18,000/year (2025 limit) per recipient.
- 529 College Plans: Fund education tax efficiently.
- Incentive trusts: Tie distributions to education, entrepreneurship, or service milestones.

Tip: Frame gifts not as entitlements but as tools for opportunity.

Giving to Charity

Be tax smart and purpose driven:

- Donate appreciated assets, specifically low cost-basis stock you own in your company: Avoid capital gains and get full deduction.
- Lifetime giving vs. bequests: Giving during life allows you to see your impact.

- Use Qualified Charitable Distributions (QCDs): After age 70½, direct IRA Required Minimum Distributions to charity. Your savings in taxes might equal the value of the distribution.

One client created a giving circle with his adult children, granting $100,000/year to causes they selected together. It led to deeper conversations and purpose alignment.

Step 5: Redefine Legacy and Success

At this stage, traditional goals shift

- From net worth to meaning,
- From asset growth to asset use, and
- From success to significance.

Explore these questions:

- What story will my wealth tell about me?
- How do I want to be remembered?
- What values do I want to see carried forward in my family?

Worksheet: Write Your Legacy Letter

- Address it to your children or future generations.
- Share your core values, lessons learned, hopes, and how you hope they'll use the resources left to them.
- Leave this letter with your will and find ways of sharing some of these thoughts and lessons during your lifetime.

Clients who complete this often say it's the most meaningful document in their entire estate plan.

Case Study: The Joy of Legacy

Jennifer established a STEM scholarship fund at her alma mater. She mentored three young women each year. She began volunteering as a science tutor at an underserved middle school. Five years later, she said, "I thought I was just giving money. But it gave me back my identity."

She wasn't just wealthy—she was joyful, connected, and living on purpose.

Final Thoughts

The greatest investment you'll ever make is in what lasts beyond you.

You've worked hard to build success. Now it's time to make it significant. Whether that means giving, mentoring, creating, or simply being present with the people you love—purpose is what makes wealth truly matter.

Let your wealth be a reflection of who you are, not just what you've earned. That's the real executive edge.

10

LEAD WITH CONFIDENCE, LIVE WITH PURPOSE

YOU'VE REACHED THE FINAL CHAPTER OF this book—but not the end of your journey. If anything, this is just the beginning.

Throughout these pages, we've explored the unique financial world of executives: the complexity of equity compensation, the tax traps and timing strategies that define high-income planning, the need to diversify intelligently, the value of estate planning that reflects your values, and the power of coordinated decision-making through an Efficient Family Office. We discussed the emotional and psychological transition to a work-optional life, and how to align wealth with purpose—not just performance.

You've learned how to take command of your wealth.

Now, it's time to lead with it.

Success Isn't the Finish Line

As an executive, you've likely spent the better part of your adult life focused on achievement. Promotions, milestones, metrics, titles—they've all served as markers of success. And financially, that success has translated into compensation, bonuses, stock options, and assets that many only dream of attaining.

But here's the truth that few talk about: Financial success alone doesn't guarantee peace of mind. It doesn't automatically bring clarity. And it certainly doesn't eliminate the pressure you feel to provide, protect, and plan wisely for the future.

If anything, wealth often brings more complexity—and with it, more responsibility.

Executives often find themselves in a quiet tension. You're supposed to "have it all together," but you're juggling a dozen financial decisions with high stakes and little time. You're managing a team, flying cross-country, sitting on boards, and trying to figure out when to exercise options, how to offset taxes, and whether your estate plan still applies.

This book has been your guide through that complexity. But more than that, it's been an invitation to pause. To reflect. To recognize that wealth, in all its dimensions, is a tool—not a destination.

From Accumulation to Alignment

The shift from building wealth to *aligning* it with your values is one of the most powerful—and underappreciated—transitions an executive can make.

When your financial life is organized, proactive, and reflective of what matters most to you, something extraordinary happens: Anxiety drops. Clarity rises. Confidence grows.

You move from reactive to intentional. You stop being "behind" on your planning and start feeling in control of it.

That's not just financial progress. That's freedom.

One of the most fulfilling aspects of my career has been helping clients make this shift. I've seen the difference in the way they show up for their families, the way they lead at work, and the way they carry themselves in the face of uncertainty. And it doesn't take a nine-figure net worth to get there. It takes intention, structure, and follow-through.

You Are the CEO of Your Financial Life

Throughout this book, you've heard me refer to your financial life as a business. That's not just a metaphor—it's a mindset.

Your wealth deserves the same attention, coordination, and strategy that you give to your career. You've managed P&Ls, built cross-functional teams, and made million-dollar decisions for your company. Now it's time to do the same for your personal balance sheet.

- **Your investments are your capital allocation decisions.**
- **Your estate plan is your long-term succession strategy.**
- **Your charitable giving is your values in action.**
- **Your team of professionals is your executive committee.**

Leading your financial life like a business doesn't mean obsessing over every detail. It means building a system that works without your constant attention—so you can focus on what matters most.

The Power of a Family Office Mindset

You've now seen how, even without hundreds of millions of dollars, you can build your own version of a family office—a model that coordinates your professionals, aligns your decisions, and provides a centralized view of your financial world.

This isn't just a luxury—it's a necessity in today's complex financial environment.

By implementing an Efficient Family Office approach, you reduce duplication, prevent mistakes, and save precious time. More importantly, you create *capacity*—the freedom to focus on your relationships, your health, your personal goals, and your purpose.

The most successful clients I work with don't have fewer responsibilities. They've just built better systems around them. They delegate wisely, stay engaged where it matters, and lead their financial life with clarity.

You can do the same.

Defining Your Legacy, Not Just Your Net Worth

A question I often ask clients near retirement is this: What story will your wealth tell about you?

Will it speak of stress, confusion, and missed opportunities? Or will it tell a story of stewardship, impact, and intention?

The way you manage your wealth sends a message to your children, your spouse, your colleagues, and your community. It reflects your priorities. It shapes your legacy.

Whether you plan to leave a financial inheritance, fund causes you care about, or simply enjoy your life with generosity and joy, your wealth has the power to do far more than grow. It can reflect who you are.

But that only happens if you take the lead.

It's Time to Act

If there's one theme that runs through every chapter of this book, it's this: **Procrastination is expensive.**

Not just in dollars but in peace of mind, opportunity cost, and emotional burden.

That unreviewed estate plan? It could mean unnecessary taxes or misaligned outcomes.

That unexercised stock option? It could expire worthless.

That unchecked concentration risk? It could derail your financial future overnight.

That charitable plan you keep putting off? It could be an opportunity lost to make a real impact—and involve your family in a shared mission.

Taking command of your wealth means moving from knowledge to action. It means no longer letting time, complexity, or uncertainty be excuses.

You don't need to do everything at once. But you do need to start.

Your Action Plan from Here

To help you move forward, here are the top ten actions I recommend to every executive after finishing this book, most of which should be done with your financial advisor:

1. **Assemble your advisory team.**
   Get your CPA, financial advisor, estate attorney, and insurance pro on the same page and let them know you are looking to do the following steps.

2. **Conduct a full financial diagnostic.**
   Ask your financial advisor to review your assets, liabilities, income sources, equity compensation, and estate documents.

3. **Build or revisit your personal net worth statement.**
   Know where you are before you decide where to go. If you have a good financial advisor or CPA, they should be able to help you with this or do it for you.

4. **Create your executive equity compensation timeline.**
   Track vesting dates, expiration windows, and planned exercises.

5. **Run a multi-year tax projection.**
   Don't wait until April—plan today for tomorrow's opportunities.

6. **Reduce overconcentration.**
   Use 10b5-1 plans, charitable giving, or exchange funds to diversify wisely.

7. **Draft or update your estate plan.**
   Make sure it reflects your current goals, family, and asset structure.

8. **Write your legacy letter.**
   Share your values, vision, and lessons with future generations.

9. **Set up a Donor-Advised Fund.**
   Make generosity part of your tax strategy and your family culture.

10. **Schedule a strategic planning retreat.**
    Whether solo or with your family, set aside time annually to review and refine your vision.

You're Not Alone

I know how hard it can be to find trustworthy, high-level advice that's actually tailored to your unique situation. That's why I wrote this book—not to sell services, but to serve leaders who often feel underserved.

But I also know this: No book can answer every question, and no plan is static. That's why I invite you to reach out.

Whether you have questions about your personal strategy, want feedback on your existing plan, or have a story to share about how you've taken command of your wealth—I'd love to hear from you.

Your experience may help another executive start their own transformation. And your decision to take action may inspire someone else to do the same.

You can connect with me directly through my firm, Kathmere Capital Management by visiting *www.kathmere.com* or emailing me at *nolesen@kathmere.com.*

This Is Your Moment

You've built an extraordinary career. You've led teams, created value, and made difficult decisions under pressure. You've earned every bit of success you've achieved.

Now it's time to lead in a new way—with your wealth.

It's time to bring the same intentionality you've brought to your career into your personal financial life. It's time to lead your family, your legacy, and your future with purpose.

This isn't about having it all figured out. It's about taking the right next step.

Start small. Be consistent. Get help where needed. And always remember: Your wealth is not just a measure of what you've earned—it's a reflection of what you can empower, enable, and inspire.

Final Words

Let this be your inflection point.

From complexity to clarity.

From reactivity to confidence.

From wealth as a burden to wealth as a blessing.

Thank you for allowing me to walk this journey with you.

Now—go live it.

Command your wealth.
Lead with clarity.
Live with purpose.

GLOSSARY OF TERMS

TO HELP YOU MAKE SOME SENSE of the alphabet soup of the financial industry, I have included this glossary of terms and a bit of information about their practical applications.

ACA/CAA

You might see ACA and CAA mentioned together when talking about healthcare. The Affordable Care Act (ACA) and Consolidated Appropriations Act (CAA) impact how employers offer and manage health coverage—especially around what's covered, what's disclosed, and how much things cost. It matters more than you'd think when planning benefits or understanding what your company provides.

AMT, Alternative Minimum Tax

The AMT is a kind of "shadow" tax system designed to make sure high earners pay at least a minimum level of tax. If you've exercised stock options or claimed large deductions, you might be surprised to find yourself paying AMT. I've helped many executives navigate this tax, which often shows up when they least expect it.

CFP®, Certified Financial Planner

This is a designation I've earned, and it reflects my commitment to always act in your best interest. It means I've gone through rigorous training, passed tough exams, and follow a code of ethics—so when I give advice, it's built on both expertise and integrity.

CPA, Certified Public Accountant

A CPA is more than just a tax preparer. They are licensed professionals trained in accounting, taxes, audits, and more. Many of my clients rely on a trusted CPA to handle both their business and personal returns, especially as their financial lives become more complex.

CPWA®, Certified Private Wealth Advisor

The CPWA® is another certification I hold, focused on serving high-net-worth individuals. It covers advanced planning strategies—think tax planning, estate structuring, and charitable giving—that go beyond the basics most advisors offer.

CRT, Charitable Remainder Trust

If you're charitably inclined but want income now and tax benefits, too, a CRT might be for you. You place assets in a trust, get income during your lifetime, and then the remainder goes to a charity you care about. It's a great way to give with intention while still taking care of yourself or your family.

DAF, Donor-Advised Fund

A DAF is one of my favorite tools for clients who want to give strategically. You donate to the fund, take a tax deduction right away, and then decide later which charities to support. It's flexible, easy to use, and a powerful way to build a giving legacy.

ESG, Environmental, Social, and Governance

ESG investing is all about aligning your portfolio with your values. If you care about causes such as sustainability, social justice, or ethical governance, ESG screens can help you invest in companies that reflect those priorities.

ESPP, Employee Stock Purchase Plan

If your employer offers an ESPP, you can buy company stock at a discount using your paycheck. For many of my clients, it's an easy way to invest in the company—just make sure you understand the tax implications when you sell.

ETF, Exchange-Traded Funds

ETFs are like a basket of investments you can buy and sell on the stock market, often with low fees and broad diversification. I often recommend them for clients who want efficient, low-cost exposure to different parts of the market.

FEIE, Foreign Earned Income Exclusion

If you work abroad, the FEIE can help you exclude a good chunk of that income from US taxes. I've worked with a number of globally mobile executives who rely on this to keep their tax bill in check.

Fiduciary

Being a fiduciary means I'm legally and ethically required to put your interests ahead of my own—always. In practice, that means every recommendation I make is based on what's best for you, not what pays me more or is easier for me. I see it as the foundation of real trust in our relationship, and it's one of the biggest differences between advisors who sell products and those who truly serve clients.

FMV, Fair Market Value

This is just the price someone would reasonably pay for something on the open market. It's important when gifting stock, exercising options, or valuing your business—and can have big tax implications.

FTC, Foreign Tax Credit

If you pay taxes to another country, the Foreign Tax Credit can help you avoid paying taxes twice on the same income. I often see this come up with clients who have overseas investments or dual citizenship.

GRAT, Grantor Retained Annuity Trust

A GRAT is an advanced estate planning tool that lets you pass wealth to your heirs with minimal tax. You keep an income stream for a few years, and then the rest goes to your kids, often with very little gift tax.

HSA, Health Savings Account

If you have a high-deductible health plan, you can use an HSA to save pre-tax money for medical expenses. It's one of the only accounts that's tax-free going in, growing, and coming out—a triple win.

ILIT, Irrevocable Life Insurance Trust

An ILIT owns a life insurance policy so that the death benefit doesn't count as part of your taxable estate. It's especially helpful for clients with large estates who want to pass on wealth efficiently.

IPO, Initial Public Offering

An IPO is when a private company becomes publicly traded. If you work at a company going public, your stock options or RSUs may finally be worth real money, but the tax and planning issues get complicated fast.

IRMAA, Income-Related Monthly Adjustment Amount

If your income is high, you'll pay extra on your Medicare premiums—that's IRMAA. It kicks in based on your income from two years ago, so planning ahead can make a big difference.

ISO, Incentive Stock Option

ISOs are stock options with special tax advantages. If you hold the shares long enough after exercising, your gains may be taxed at lower capital gains rates. But they also come with AMT risk, so timing matters.

KPI, Key Performance Indicator

KPIs are just the metrics you measure to see if you're on track—like revenue growth, profit margins, or new client acquisitions. I use KPIs in both my business and when helping clients measure progress toward their goals.

NIIT, Net Investment Income Tax

If you earn above certain thresholds, you'll owe an extra 3.8% tax on investment income like dividends, capital gains, and interest. It's a sneaky tax that often catches high earners off guard.

NSO, Non-Qualified Stock Options

NSOs don't get the same tax benefits as ISOs. When you exercise them, you owe ordinary income tax on the difference between the strike price and the market value. Still, they can be valuable if managed well.

PE, Private Equity

PE firms invest in private companies with the goal of scaling them up and eventually selling at a profit. For clients with PE exposure—either directly or through funds—it can be a big source of wealth creation (and complexity).

PFIC, Passive Foreign Investment Companies

If you own a foreign mutual fund or offshore investment, it may be classified as a PFIC, which comes with harsh tax rules. These are landmines in disguise—always worth checking with a tax pro before investing internationally.

POD, Payable on Death

Adding a POD designation to a bank account lets it go directly to your chosen beneficiary when you pass—no probate needed. It's a simple, effective estate planning move.

PSU, Performance Stock Units

PSUs are shares you earn only if your company hits specific goals like growing earnings or hitting stock price targets. They're often used to align executive compensation with company performance.

QCD, Qualified Charitable Distribution

A QCD lets you donate directly from your IRA to a charity, and it counts toward your Required Minimum Distribution (RMD) without adding to your taxable income. If you're over 70½, this is one of my favorite strategies to reduce your tax bill and support causes you care about. I often suggest QCDs to clients who are already giving generously but don't need the extra income from their IRA. It's a simple way to give smarter, not just more.

REIT, Real Estate Investment Trust

REITs let you invest in real estate without becoming a landlord. They're required to pay out most of their income as dividends, making them attractive to income-focused investors.

RMD, Required Minimum Distribution

Once you hit a certain age (currently 73), the IRS requires you to start taking money out of your retirement accounts. Miss the deadline, and the penalties are steep, so we always plan these in advance.

RSU, Restricted Stock Unit

RSUs are company shares you earn over time—usually tied to how long you stay or how the company performs. Once they vest, they're considered income, and you can sell or hold them like regular stock.

SBLOC, Securities-Backed Line of Credit

An SBLOC lets you borrow against your investment account without selling your holdings. It's handy for short-term needs, like a real estate purchase, but must be managed carefully to avoid risk during market drops.

TOD, Transfer on Death

Similar to POD, a TOD designation applies to investment accounts and lets you name a beneficiary who receives the assets directly when you pass. It's an easy way to bypass probate and ensure a smooth transfer.

VC, Venture Capital

VC investors fund startups with high growth potential—think early-stage tech companies. If you're offered equity in a startup, you're essentially getting a slice of VC-style risk and potential reward.

ACKNOWLEDGMENTS

THIS BOOK IS AS MUCH A reflection of the incredible team at Kathmere Capital Management as it is a guide for executives seeking financial clarity. From the beginning, Kathmere has been built on the belief that wealth management should be deeply personal, remarkably thoughtful, and always aligned with the values of those we serve. It's not just about managing assets—it's about stewarding a family's future with intention, clarity, and care.

To my partners and colleagues at Kathmere, your dedication to these principles inspires me every day. You've embraced the vision of putting clients first, of challenging the status quo in our industry, and of crafting strategies that honor not just financial goals, but life goals. Your commitment to excellence, collaboration, and genuine care has made Kathmere a firm that stands apart.

Thank you for believing in the power of integrated, purpose-driven advice. Thank you for pouring your talents into the families we serve. This book would not exist without the collective wisdom, diligence, and heart of this team.

To our clients, thank you. Thank you for entrusting us with your most important decisions, for allowing us a seat at the table as you navigate careers, family legacies, transitions, and aspirations. The relationships we've built are more than professional; they are partnerships grounded in trust and mutual respect. Your openness, your stories, and your desire for clarity have shaped the way we approach our craft.

And on a personal note, to my incredible kids. Thank you for your life-giving love and for the joy you bring in simply wanting to be with your dad, the greatest title and calling I could ever have, on this adventure we share. You are the reason I relentlessly pursue these dreams and work so hard to provide and build this life for us. I love you deeply and am more proud of each of you than words could ever capture. I promise I will always show up, always cheer the loudest, and always be your biggest fan. Choose joy. Help others. Be kind. And never forget, God has blessed us beyond measure.

ABOUT THE AUTHOR

NICHOLAS J.D. OLESEN, CFP®, CPWA®, IS a Founding Principal at Kathmere Capital Management, where he specializes in guiding executives, business owners, and their families through the complexities of wealth management.

Nicholas advises some of the firm's key private wealth relationships and sits on the investment committee. With two decades of experience, Nicholas has built a reputation for helping high-income earners achieve financial clarity and align their wealth with what matters most.

Nicholas is a trusted advisor to clients across the country, including executives at Fortune 100 companies, offering sophisticated, highly customized financial strategies that reflect each client's unique circumstances. Known for his discretion, clarity, and steady leadership, Nicholas is often described as both a confidant and a strategic partner in his clients' lives.

Nicholas's financial insights have been featured in prominent outlets including The Wall Street Journal, CNBC, Financial Times, USA Today, SmartMoney, Thomson Reuters, and Philadelphia Business Journal. His perspective is frequently sought out for commentary on investment strategy, executive compensation, tax-efficient planning, and multigenerational wealth management.

Nicholas holds a Bachelor of Science in Economics from James Madison University and maintains both the Certified Financial Planner™ (CFP®) and Certified Private Wealth Advisor® (CPWA®) designations. He earned the CPWA® after completing an intensive executive education program at The University of Chicago Booth School of Business, designed for elite advisors serving high-net-worth individuals and families.

Nicholas and his energetic children can be found exploring new hiking trails and adventures, playing countless sports, rooting for the Phillies and Packers, or making homemade pizzas. As Steve Jobs said, “Your time is limited, so don’t waste it living someone else’s life.”

LET'S START A CONVERSATION

Wealth brings complexity. But it also brings opportunity, opportunity to align your finances with your life's purpose, to protect what matters most, and to create clarity in areas that often feel overwhelming.

If the strategies and perspectives in this book resonate with you, I invite you to take the next step. Whether you're navigating equity compensation, preparing for a major transition, or simply looking for a more intentional approach to managing your wealth, my team and I at Kathmere Capital Management are here to help.

Our work is built on relationships, not transactions. We partner with executives, business owners, and families who want more than generic advice. They want clarity. They want a plan. They want a trusted team that understands their unique path and will walk alongside them.

If that sounds like you, I would love to hear your story.

Reach out to me directly:

Nicholas Olesen, CFP®, CPWA®

nolesen@kathmere.com

www.kathmere.com

Let's start a conversation about how we can help you command your wealth—with clarity, purpose, and confidence.

www.ingramcontent.com/pod-product-compliance
Lightning Source LLC
LaVergne TN
LVHW050916210926
848482LV00012B/466
* 9 7 9 8 9 9 9 7 8 2 2 0 5 *